TIGERS

First published in Great Britain in 1996 by
Colin Baxter Photography Ltd.,
Grantown-on-Spey,
Moray PH26 3NA
Scotland

Reprinted 1998, 2000, 2002, 2004

A CIP Catalogue record for this book is available from the British Library

ISBN 0-948661-88-7

Photographs © 1996:

Front cover © Martin Harvey (NHPA)
Back cover © Andy Rouse (NHPA)
Page 1 © Terry Whittaker (FLPA)
Page 4 © Martin Harvey (NHPA)
Page 6 © Jean-Pierre Zwaenepoel (Bruce Coleman Ltd)
Page 8 © Andy Rouse (NHPA)
Page 9 © Martin Harvey (NHPA)
Page 10 © Gunter Ziesler (Bruce Coleman Ltd)
Page 13 © Mahipal Singh (Oxford Scientific Films)
Page 14 © Jean-Pierre Zwaenepoel (Bruce Coleman Ltd)
Page 16 © Jean-Pierre Zwaenepoel (Bruce Coleman Ltd)
Page 17 © T Whittaker (FLPA)
Page 18 © Alain Compost (Bruce Coleman Ltd)
Page 19 © Alain Compost (Bruce Coleman Ltd)
Page 20 © Erwin and Peggy Bauer (Bruce Coleman Ltd)
Page 23 © Andy Rouse (NHPA)
Page 24 © Jean-Pierre Zwaenepoel (Bruce Coleman Ltd)
Page 27 © Christer Fredriksson (Bruce Coleman Ltd)
Page 28 © Fiona Sunquist
Page 29 © Fiona Sunquist
Page 31 © S Nagaraj (Oxford Scientific Films)
Page 32 © Mahipal Singh (Oxford Scientific Films)

Page 35 © Gunter Ziesler (Bruce Coleman Ltd)
Page 36 © Mahipal Singh (Oxford Scientific Films)
Page 39 © Andy Rouse (NHPA)
Page 40 © Jean-Pierre Zwaenepoel (Bruce Coleman Ltd)
Page 43 © Vivek Sinha (Survival Anglia)
Page 44 © Gunter Ziesler (Bruce Coleman Ltd)
Page 45 © Jean-Pierre Zwaenepoel (Bruce Coleman Ltd)
Page 47 © Andy Rouse (NHPA)
Page 48 © Jean-Pierre Zwaenepoel (Bruce Coleman Ltd)
Page 51 © Mahipal Singh (Oxford Scientific Films)
Page 52 © Gerard Lacz (NHPA)
Page 55 © Andy Rouse (NHPA)
Page 57 © Martin Harvey (NHPA)
Page 58 © Gunter Ziesler (Bruce Coleman Ltd)
Page 61 © Belinda Wright (Oxford Scientific Films)
Page 62 © Jean-Pierre Zwaenepoel (Bruce Coleman Ltd)
Page 65 © Andy Rouse (NHPA)
Page 66 © Jean-Pierre Zwaenepoel (Bruce Coleman Ltd)
Page 68 © Belinda Wright (Oxford Scientific)
Page 69 © Erwin and Peggy Bauer (Bruce Coleman Ltd)
Page 70 © Jean-Pierre Zwaenepoel (Bruce Coleman Ltd)

Printed in China

TIGERS

John Seidensticker

Colin Baxter Photography, Grantown-on-Spey, Scotland

Contents

Tigers   Page 7

Origins   Page 15

Ways of Knowing   Page 25

Predator and Prey   Page 33

Family Life   Page 53

Saving the Tiger   Page 67

Tiger Facts   Page 71

Tigers

The tiger lives in a world of sunlight and shadow
Always secretive – never devious
Always a killer – never a murderer
Solitary – never alone
For it is an irreplaceable link
In the process and the wholeness of life.

I wrote those words in the fall of 1974 while I was studying tiger predation and predatory behavior in Nepal's Royal Chitwan National Park. During several months of daily tiger encounters, real tigers living their lives, often within the sounds of busy village life, I found tigers so unlike the tiger depicted in the oft-quoted William Blake poem "The Tyger" (*Tyger! Tyger! burning bright / In the forests of the night / What immortal hand or eye / Dare frame thy fearful symmetry?*). Hearing a tiger roaring in the night or seeing a tiger track on a dusty forest road brings a sense of power and tension and grace to a landscape that only the largest predators can invoke.

In our rapidly changing world, the endangered tiger's decline represents real and symbolic loss of quality of life. Landscapes where the endangered tiger and people live together, and the tiger and its living area are viewed and supported as a positive feature in the landscape, are landscapes to be treasured, as are the lessons to be learned from them. The continued survival of the tiger completely depends on this. To me, landscapes where tigers live today represent the highest levels of ecological integrity and ecological completeness, the very existence of which reaches into and affects the quality of our own lives.

There is something special about tigers that evokes strong feelings in nearly everyone. For anyone living in tiger-land, special care is always taken when moving about to avoid surprise encounters. For the armchair traveller, just thinking about tigers conjures up images of lush jungles in exotic far-off lands. Tigers are among the most recognisable of all animals, embodying great power, lithe and awesome grace, mystery, stealth, and danger. Tigers serve as symbols of freedom and nature untouched. Tigers are the steeds of gods.

In Hinduism, the god Shiva is both destroyer and reproducer. As destroyer, he is pictured wearing a tiger skin and riding a tiger. His consort is Parvati the Beautiful, who, in her dark side, appears as Durga the Terrible, riding a tiger. In some Asian cultures, tigers

incarnate mystery and potentially dangerous beings. Shamans and magicians adopt the guise of tigers to promote powerful images. Tigers are believed to be the avengers of their Supreme Being or to punish sinners on behalf of Allah.

In ancient China, tigers were considered regal and beneficial during some periods. At other times they were regarded as potent messengers between the human and spirit worlds. In still other periods, tiger images were used to deter evil spirits from the graves of the deceased. A tiger, sleeping or sitting at the feet of monks, demonstrates Buddhism's power to harmonise and tame nature's forces. A roaring tiger symbolises a fury and fighting spirit. Tigers and dragons together symbolise the two great forces of nature. In Taoism *yin,* or evil, is controlled by the tiger and the dragon controls *yang,* or good. The role of the tiger is reversed in Buddhist thought, in which the tiger represents *yang.*

Just watching a tiger walking down a forest road or patrolling the edge of a moat in a zoological park, you can see that everything about its movements speaks of an easy power and grace. In a blink, a tiger can recast into an awesome killing machine. Muscles tensed in a stalk, an explosive rush, abrupt turn, graceful leap, unanticipated stop, the tiger's great size amplifies our perception of its agility. We see the motions we expect in a

Forest surrounding the abandoned fort at Ranthambhore, India, provides a rare opportunity for tigers to replace people in the landscape. In most of the tiger's once vast range, people now predominate at the tiger's expense.

house cat, only one per cent of a tiger's size.

Tigers are the largest of 36 species of living cats. Once widespread and abundant over their vast range in southern and eastern Asia, tigers lived in habitats including rain forests, mangroves, scrub and thorn forests, forests and tall grass areas on river flood plains, and even in the temperate forests of the Russian Far East. In addition to cover and water to drink and cool off in, this largest cat needs large mammalian prey to survive. The tiger is a specialised predator of large hoofed mammals (ungulates). Large deer, such as the sambar and red deer, and wild swine are mainstays in their diet throughout their range. They also prey on wild cattle, such as gaur and banteng, where they occur in the southern reaches of their range. Tigers also kill domestic cattle and buffalo where these are made available to them in their habitat. Occasionally, tigers kill people.

For much of this century, ridding a region of tigers was considered a sign of progress and a step on a path to positive economic development. No one gave much thought to what the world would be like without tigers. Describing the Sundarbans, the magnificent mangrove forests at the mouths of the Ganges where it interfaces with Bay of Bengal in India and Bangladesh and one of the largest expanses of tiger habitat remaining today, E. E. Baker wrote in 1887: "The sole distinctive characteristic of this tiger, so far as is known, is its utter fearlessness of man, and its inveterate propensity to kill and devour him on all and every opportunity." Writing a management plan for the tiger and other wildlife in the Bangladesh coastal zone nearly a century later, my colleague M. A. Hai and I concluded: "The survival in the wild of the powerful metaphysical symbol of Bangladesh, the royal Bengal tiger, hinges upon the capability and the will of man. In the Sundarbans, tigers, deer, forest, and men are linked inseparably and so must be their management. Any attempt to separate the tiger from its prey, the deer from the forest, or people from their needs will surely fail. The tiger must be managed with all wildlife as an integral part of forest management that ensures the sustainable production of forest products and maintains this coastal zone at the level of best achievable ecosystem function to provide for the needs of the people of Bangladesh." And so it is throughout the tiger's range today.

It comes down to this: the largest of the cats, the predator powerful enough to kill all but the very largest of mammals, is endangered. Endangered means that if present trends continue as they are now, the tiger will become extinct in the wild. Most experts agree that, even with more than two decades of intensive international and national efforts to conserve tigers, they are worse off today than when their endangered plight was first recognised in the late 1960s.

Two events have brought the tiger to the brink. First, there has been a massive reduction in suitable tiger habitat throughout its range since the end of World War II, as more and more former wildlands have been turned to agricultural production to support our ever expanding human population. Further, what remains of tiger habitat has been divided again and again and the tiger population as a whole has been divided into smaller and smaller fractions, a process called fragmentation, until there are no longer any large expanses of tiger habitat left or any large populations of tigers left living in any one area.

Second, people have continued killing tigers. There are a few legitimate reasons for removing a problem tiger now and then, such as insuring the personal safety of people living in tiger areas or to reduce depredation on livestock. However, concerted efforts to stop a massive haemorrhage in tiger numbers from illegal killing for their elegant fur and as a source of tiger parts and products for traditional medicine makers, supplying increasingly demanding and affluent markets, have not been successful. So, even in many regions where there are areas of suitable tiger habitat, tiger numbers are greatly reduced, or the tiger is no longer present.

Is the tiger doomed in the wild? The tiger is certainly "On the Brink", as *Time* magazine shouted in a 1995 cover story. Leading conservationist and USA Secretary of Interior Bruce Babbitt put the chilling fact this way: "There may not be another chance to save the tiger." If our collective attitude towards the tiger is one of antipathy and intolerance the tiger will disappear from the wild. This would be a terrible loss, symbolising a morbid disregard for natural places and wildlife conservation in general. The tiger's future rests in our hands and is completely dependent on our awareness of its plight and upon the level of support we provide for its survival.

Origins

In technical reports, scientists usually refer to the tiger as *Panthera tigris*. The first word, *Panthera*, is the genus, or group of closely related species, that the tiger belongs to. The genus name is sometimes abbreviated to *P*. Other species in the genus *Panthera* are the lion (*P. leo*), the leopard (*P. pardus*), and the jaguar (*P. onca*). The second word, *tigris*, is the species name. Together, the genus and species name form a unique combination to identify a unique species of animal. A species consists of a population or series of populations of similar and closely related individuals that breed freely and produce live young with one another but not with other species, even ones in the same genus, under natural conditions.

Scientific names are usually from Greek or Latin words. This system, called the binomial (two-word) system, was invented by the Swedish naturalist Carolus Linnaeus in the 1700s. Why do scientists use this system? First, it avoids confusion. To English speakers, the word tiger always means a large, orange striped cat from Asia. But to Spanish speakers in South America, el tigre means a jaguar. North Americans called their large native cat a mountain lion, but this animal is not even very closely related to the lion of Africa. What's more, there are dozens of local names for tigers in the languages of people who live among them (see Tiger Facts p 71). By using a universally agreed upon name for this animal, people will always know which animal you are talking about.

Another reason for scientific names is that they say something about how animals are related to each other. Calling all of the cats mentioned above *Panthera* shows they are more closely related to each other than they are to other cats with different genus names. For instance, it is clear from their scientific names that tigers and lions are more closely related to each other than either is to the mountain lion, *Puma concolor*. In fact, the *Panthera* cats will interbreed and produce live hybrid young if they live together in zoos. Minor physical differences, including differences in body size and coat pattern, distinguish these species. Only a specialist could tell the difference between a lion and a tiger placed side by side without their coats.

Including the *Panthera* group, there are 36 species of cats living today. Twenty-nine species are small cats, such as wild counterparts of domestic cats, that weigh less than 20 kg (44 lb). Five are medium sized, including leopards and jaguars, that weigh between 40 and 80 kg (88 and 132 lb). Only the lion and the tiger are truly giants, tipping the scales at least 140 kg (about 300 lb) and at most up to 260 kg (about 570 lb).

These cats, called the family Felidae, together with the families that include bears, dogs, weasels, raccoons, civets, mongooses, hyenas, and a few others, belong to the mammalian order Carnivora. These animals all descended from a squirrel-sized mammal that chased insects more than 65 million years ago. In common speech, all members of the order Carnivora are called carnivores, implying that all are meat eaters. But the various carnivore families have evolved differing skull, teeth, and body adaptations that allow them to exploit different food sources and, thus, they are not all purely meat eaters. In fact, some carnivores, such as sloth bears, live almost entirely on insects and fruit, while others rely on plant material, such as the giant panda which eats mostly bamboo.

What then sets the Carnivora apart from other mammals? One important trait is that almost all members of this order possess a set of scissor-like back teeth called carnassials, which are used to cut flesh, and a set of sharply pointed canine teeth in the front of the jaw. The characteristics of these teeth are particularly pronounced in cats: all cats have strong, pointed canines set in short, powerful jaws, and their carnassials

Tigers use sharp, long canine teeth in a short, powerful jaw to grab and kill their prey.

are honed to perfection.

Scientists call cats *hypercarnivores* because their diets consist almost entirely of flesh of other vertebrates (mammals, birds, reptiles, amphibians, and fish). Omnivory – eating a mixed diet including fruits, nuts, and insects – is not an option for cats because their entire digestive system is adapted to processing meat. While meat is easier to digest than plant material and very nourishing, it comes with strings attached. Finding

prey can be difficult and catching it can be very dangerous. Thus, a strictly carnivorous diet can affect other aspects of a cat's life, including its behavior and social system, as you will see in later chapters.

The *Panthera* or "roaring" cats are specialised predators of large mammals, primarily ungulates (hoofed prey such as deer and wild pigs). They capture prey through stealth and speed and use their great strength to kill prey that are as large or larger than themselves. Killing large prey with muscular necks and massive vertebra requires special behaviors and tools, such as the canines described above. But another solution that evolved at least four times in different groups of mammals is the stabbing saber tooth. There are several extinct species of sabertooth cats, but best known is the sabertooth whose fossils are abundant in California's Rancho La Brea tarpits. This is the species, *Smilodon fatalis*, seen in so many illustrations and often mistakenly called a sabertooth tiger. But the sabertooth cats are only a primitive, distant relative of tigers, and tigers did not evolve

Living in the rain forest of this Indonesian island, Sumatran tigers are the smallest of the living tiger subspecies – about half the size of their mainland relatives.

19

Believed to be the largest of tigers, about 450 Siberian tigers inhabit the deciduous and evergreen forests of the Amur Valley in the Russian Far East.

these cats. In fact, until they became extinct about 10,000 years ago, some species of sabertooths lived at the same time and in the same places as lions and tigers.

Where did tigers come from? All of the *Panthera* cats evolved from a common ancestor that was probably fairly similar to modern leopards or jaguars and lived more than 5 million years ago. The first fossils that scientists can clearly identify as tigers are about 2 million years old. These fossils are from central Asia, eastern and northern China, Siberia, Japan, Sumatra, and Java – not too different from the modern range of tigers. Fossils found in western North America and south into northern South America confirm the existence there of very large *Panthera* cats during the last million years. Most of these fossils are considered to be lions. However, the paleontologist Sandra Herrington believes that tigers may have reached what is now Alaska during the Wisconsin glaciation (beginning about 300,000 years ago) over the Bering land bridge that then existed between Siberia and Alaska. In any case, it is clear that until about 10,000 years ago, when there were mass extinctions of large mammals in North America, lions lived throughout North America, Asia, and Africa. Tigers, however, were restricted to the forested regions of temperate and tropical Asia, as they have been in historic times.

When specimens of tigers from different areas of their range began to arrive in the great European natural history museums in the nineteenth century, the taxonomist who examined them found some interesting differences between them. While clearly all of these specimens were tigers, specimens from some areas consistently differed in certain features from specimens from other areas. To recognize these characteristic forms from different geographic areas, taxonomists described them as subspecies. Members of a subspecies share a unique geographical range or habitat, have identifiable physical characteristics, and have a unique natural history relative to other subspecies in the species. Subspecies may arise over time; for instance, the fossil lions of America are considered one subspecies of lion, and the modern lion another. Subspecies may also arise through what scientists call "geographic partitioning." This simply means that populations of animals living in different areas, usually separated by barriers such as mountain ranges or seas, evolve some different traits, but not ones that would prevent individuals from breeding successfully with one another should they come together. In fact, sometimes subspecies "collapse" when the barrier that separated them is removed. In contrast, species, such as lions and tigers, retain their identity even when they occur in the same areas in the wild. Scientists add a third word to the scientific name to indicate a subspecies. For example, fossil lions are called *Panthera leo atrox* and modern African lions *Panthera leo leo*.

Today scientists recognise eight different tiger subspecies. These are: the Bengal tiger, *Panthera tigris tigris,* from the Indian subcontinent; the now extinct Caspian tiger, *Panthera tigris virgata,* from the areas around the Caspian Sea; the Indo-Chinese tiger, *Panthera tigris corbetti,* from mainland southeast Asia; the Chinese tiger, *Panthera tigris amoyensis,* from southern and central China; the Amur or Siberian tiger, *Panthera tigris altaica,* from northeastern China, Korea, and the Russian Far East; the Sumatran tiger, *Panthera tigris sumatrae,* from the Indonesian island of Sumatra; the extinct Javan tiger, *Panthera tigris sondaica,* and the extinct Bali tiger, *Panthera tigris balica,* from the Indonesian islands of Java and Bali, respectively. The island tigers are much smaller – only about half the size – of the mainland subspecies (see Tiger Facts p 71). All of the subspecies are distinguishable based on differences in the colors and striping of their coats and in characteristic differences in their skulls. The so-called "white tigers" are just a rare color form and are not a different species or even subspecies. There are a few "black" tigers on record that all came from northeast of the Bay of Bengal. This is a color form of the Bengal tiger. The three subspecies that have become extinct have done so since the end of World War II, and there are none living in zoological parks today.

Note: Readers familiar with the scientific literature on cats may wonder what happened to the snow leopard in my discussion of *Panthera* species. For many years, the snow leopard was called *Panthera uncia*. As a result of a recent re-evaluation of the relationships between cats, however, the snow leopard has been renamed *Uncia uncia*.

Perhaps 40,000 Bengal tigers roamed the Indian subcontinent at the start of the last century. The 4000 that remain may not survive very far into the twenty-first century.

Ways of Knowing

How did we learn what we now know about tigers? How will we learn more in the future? What information is needed to save the tiger? The history of the Western-style scientific study of tigers is actually quite short. Of course, people living among tigers have long known a lot about the behavior of this beautiful, dangerous predator – their survival depended, and in some places still depends on this knowledge, just as modern city dwellers must know a lot about the behavior of people driving cars. The arts, myths, and legends of much of Asia are also replete with tiger themes.

In Europe, little was known about tigers beyond travellers' tales and their infrequent appearances in menageries. Shakespeare invoked tiger imagery, perhaps most notably in Henry V's exhortation to his men at the battle of Agincourt: "But when the blast of war blows in our ears/Then imitate the action of the tiger"; but tigers found no place in Western art or culture until quite recently.

In the 1800s, however, tiger specimens began arriving in Western natural history museums as collectors travelled the globe in search of material to send back "home." Although the killing and collecting of tigers (or any animal) may be shocking to us today, at the time obtaining such material for scientific study was an accepted, even noble, pursuit. And indeed, from these specimens we learned most of what we know about the tiger's anatomy, its geographic distribution and subspecies, and its relationship to other cats. This material, as well as specimens of tigers that died in zoological parks, still exists in museums today, available for further study as new questions arise.

To study tigers in the wild – to learn about their ecology and behavior – is not easy. Tigers hunt primarily at night, they are highly secretive, and they are dangerous. So, as George Schaller wrote in *The Deer and the Tiger*, until 1967 "…the natural history of the tiger has been studied predominately along the sights of a rifle…" Tigers sometimes kill livestock and they sometimes kill people. The Western hunters who attempted to dispatch these "problem" tigers, and who also led sport hunters on the trail of tigers, created an entire literature based on their exploits. These accounts describe searching for and killing tigers (and sometimes being killed by them) and reveal the insights they had into tiger behavior that made them mostly successful. This phase in our knowledge about tigers is best captured by Jim Corbett in his book *Man-Eaters of Kumaon*. Corbett depicted the drama of the conflict between people and tigers, but his writing is also filled with respect for the great cats he hunted and killed.

Whatever the value of these hunters' accounts, the information they provided about tigers was anecdotal and sometimes highly exaggerated. In 1967, George Schaller changed all that, revolutionizing the study of tigers through the application of the scientific method. Studying tigers in India, Schaller's tools were a sturdy pair of walking shoes, a Land Rover, binoculars, notebook and pen, and a certain amount of courage. He made careful, systematic observations of tigers through all the seasons of year. Further, he was able to identify individual tigers and chart the course of their differing activities. From this study, Schaller was able to provide a detailed account of the behavior and ecology of wild tigers living in central India. In splendid prose, he introduced us to the world of living, breathing, roaring, hunting, mating, and cub-rearing tigers that strongly contrasted with the often savage portraits painted by hunters.

As Schaller finished his study, another compelling reason to study tigers scientifically emerged. At the 1969 meeting of the World Conservation Union (IUCN) in New Delhi, India, five very senior conservationists – Salim Ali, Zafar Futehally, J.C. Daniel, Guy Mountfort, and S. Dillon Ripley – stood together to express their deep concern about the tiger's survival in India and throughout its range. They observed that the landscape in tiger-land was rapidly changing and the tiger – once regarded as too powerful and too able to deal with change ever to be vulnerable – was disappearing from its old haunts. Where until World War II and even after, tigers were commonly encountered, there were none. If tigers were to survive, they said, something had to be done. As a result, three years later, a "Save the Tiger" program was launched to raise funds, generate international public support, and encourage governments within the tiger's range to begin conservation action programs, including creating reserves for tigers.

A first order of business was to find out where and how many tigers still lived. In India, this task fell to Kailash Sankhala. He organised teams of tiger counters to fan through the

Safe and effective drugs allow scientists to capture and safely attach a radio collar to a tiger. Radio telemetry is the only way to study such a large, dangerous and secretive denizen of densely vegetated habitats.

forests of India to find where tigers lived and in about what numbers. For the first time, there was good information on the distribution of tigers in India, and this information was used by the government to set up a special reserve system for the protection of tigers.

As Schaller first demonstrated, the ability to identify individual tigers is essential. Only by knowing who's who, can you learn how the tigers in a particular area interact with one another, what factors influence a tiger's ability to raise offspring, and how young tigers, after leaving their mothers, search for and succeed — or fail — in finding new places to live in changing landscapes and shrinking habitats.

Once a tiger is radio collared, scientists can follow its activities from afar.

In Nepal, in the early 1970s, Charles McDougal learned to tell tigers apart by their face marks, and further, by their pug marks, or tracks, as tigers are not always willing to reveal their faces. Following these tracks and watching known tigers at kills, coupled with the ingenious use of "camera traps" rigged to automatically photograph tigers passing by, McDougal has been able to document the lives of some individual tigers with more precision and for longer periods of time than anyone else has achieved (see Family Life p 53). His work continues to this day.

Also in the early 1970s, the Smithsonian Institution joined forces with His Majesty's Government of Nepal and applied a potent mixture of old and new technologies to studying tigers in the wild. The old: elephants, specially trained to closely approach tigers, and direct observation when possible. The new: dart guns loaded with drugs to immobilise tigers so that a radio collar could be put on and radio-tracking equipment used to find and follow tigers at a distance and throughout their lives. Using these tools, teams of researchers, led at different times by myself, Hemanta Mishra, David Smith, Melvin Sunquist, and Kirti Man Tamang, have been able to assess what a tiger needs at each stage of its life. In turn, this detailed information suggests how to resolve conflicts between tigers and people and how to plan the reserve system that tigers need to survive in their changing, shrinking habitats.

Most recently, powerful computers and satellites have been added to the tiger-studying tool chest. David Smith and Ronald Tilson, for example, are using information gathered by satellites and analysed in Geographic Information Systems computer models to find out how much and where habitat for tigers still exists. Ullas Karanth and Tilson are working on better ways to tell tigers apart so highly accurate counts of tiger populations in various areas can be made quickly. Even today, with all we know about tigers, the answer to such a seemingly simple question as "How many are there?" is an educated guess, but one with profound consequences. With only 4,700 to 7,700 tigers in total, a guess on the high side might lead to false complacency about a particular tiger population's future, while one on the low side might lead to a population being wrongly "written-off" as too far gone to save.

On other fronts, Stephen O'Brien and his associates are applying sophisticated DNA testing to blood and skin samples (collected remotely with special darts) to tell how closely related the tigers in a population are and to assess the potential risk of various diseases breaking out. This work may provide an early warning of dangerous levels of inbreeding or lurking disease. Both of these are serious potential hazards to tigers living in small, isolated populations. David Wildt and JoGayle Howard have added to our understanding of the reproductive physiology of tigers, pioneering methods of artificial insemination and producing "test-tube" baby tigers that might one day be used to reduce inbreeding problems in tiger populations. Finally, zoo biologists, using all that is now known about the natural history of tigers, have developed breeding programs to maintain healthy tiger populations in zoos. These populations offer insurance against the risk of losing tigers entirely in the wild and help educate people about their plight.

Our ways of knowing about tigers continue to progress. We hope this growing knowledge is enough and in time to keep tigers a part of wild Asia.

Predator and Prey

The elephant Rabi Kali and her two mahouts picked me up on a late afternoon in January. Setting off from my remote research camp, I took a rocking and rolling elephant-back ride across the Rapti River and into lowland Nepal's Chitwan National Park. My goal was an isolated bombax tree, about a kilometer from the river. The tree stood near the centre of a 50-hectare (about 120 acres) patch of grass so tall – some 5 m – that even atop a huge Asian elephant I could see little but waving green stems.

Rabi Kali, however, walked purposefully down the narrow path cut through the tall grass, sidled up to the 15-m tall tree, and stopped. This was where I was to get off. I climbed from the elephant into the lower branches of the tree and scrambled onto a small platform, called a machan, barely big enough to hold me and the equipment I was encumbered with: binoculars, night-vision scope, 35-mm still camera with telephoto lens, and a radio-tracking receiver with directional antenna. As I arranged this array of expensive tools, securing each item with a short cord so a clumsy movement didn't send any of them crashing 6 m (20 ft) to the ground, Rabi Kali disappeared down the path. So quietly did she move that I could only follow her trail by glimpses of her mahout's head occasionally bobbing above the tall grass. Alone, I made myself comfortable in the 1-m (10 ft) square tree platform and waited.

This was an important night. I had come to Chitwan in 1972 with my Nepalese colleague Kirti Man Tamang to initiate the Nepal-Smithsonian Tiger Ecology Project. Our goal was to develop a detailed portrait of tiger ecology and behavior by combining old and new technologies. Our primary transport and tiger-catching "machine" were trained elephants, carefully conditioned to approach tigers in this dense habitat. Riding these elephants, we could closely approach tigers, dart them with immobilising drugs, attach radio collars, then follow their movements by radio day and night for years. As much direct observation as the tigers allowed would supplement the data we collected remotely. Such an approach was essential to studying the dangerous, secretive, wide-ranging tiger – but it had never been done before. Barring the elephants, I had pioneered such methods while studying mountain lions in the mountains of Idaho, USA. Now I would see how they would work in the tall grass of Nepal.

This part of Chitwan is an old, filled-in river channel, one of many created during past monsoons (rainy seasons) when the flooded Rapti River overflowed its banks and carved new channels over the valley bottom. Old winding channels, cut off from the river, turned into oxbow lakes, expanses of tall grass, and gallery forest (wooded areas along rivers). This is superb wildlife habitat, with, among other creatures, very dense populations of such tiger prey species as sambar (a large Asian deer), axis deer, hog deer, wild pigs, and muntjac. In addition, about 350 greater one-horned rhinoceros live here. We now know that each square kilometer of this area supports about 70 individual animals a tiger can prey on, and therefore supports one of the most dense tiger populations known today.

Chitwan is one of the finest of Nepal's – and all of Asia's – national parks but the sights and sounds of village life are all around. From my machan, looking north of the river just outside the park, I could see trails of dust rising from cattle and water buffalo being driven to village compounds for the night. I could hear the regular *tut-tut-tut* of a rice mill. Off to the east, just over a ditch-fence that formed a park boundary, women were walking home, loads of firewood and other belongings perched on their heads. All of this bustling human activity within an earshot of such superb tiger habitat is a reminder of just how intertwined the lives of tigers and people have become in today's crowded world. And this is not unique. In fact, it is the norm, and frequently results in conflicts that those who wish to conserve tigers must constantly recognise and attempt to resolve.

Turning away from the edges, I scanned the inner area with my binoculars, looking for signs of tiger prey. I saw movement 50 m (55yds) off to the south that I suspected was a rhino feeding, but I couldn't be sure as the tall grass obscured my view. Adult rhinos and elephants are too big for tigers to kill, but tigers can and do kill their calves. I watched a wild boar for a few fleeting seconds as it walked down the trail I had just come over, but it too disappeared into the grass. Then I flipped on my radio-tracking

Tigers hunt where they are most likely to find prey.
Well watered areas with tree cover are favorite haunts of
deer and pigs, and so too of tigers.

receiver and immediately picked up the signal from tigress 101. Tigress 101 was special – the first-ever wild tiger to wear a radio collar. We had put it on her a month earlier and, to our great relief, she had not taken it off.

Listening carefully to the strength and variation in the signal beeps and using the directional antenna, I could tell she was moving – and moving rapidly my way! I readied my camera just as she emerged from the grass and onto the same trail I and the wild boar had travelled. She moved with caution and an easy tension, her head held high, nose testing the air. Reaching the spot where the boar had just veered off the trail, she stopped abruptly then rushed around a large clump of grass and disappeared momentarily. But just as she made her move, the boar snorted and ran off, and tigress 101 immediately reappeared at the spot vacated by the boar. It all happened in no time, but I had learned something. It was clear that 101 had used both sound and scent to detect this boar; most earlier accounts suggested that tigers used only sight to find prey. This was the first attempted kill I'd seen and not surprisingly it was unsuccessful. Earlier researchers estimated that tigers made a kill in only one of 10 or 20 such attempts.

As I watched, the tigress tested the air then resumed her walk down the trail and paused under my tree. She was alert and appeared nervous, perhaps sensing my presence or something else that signalled caution, but she did not look up. Scarcely breathing, I snapped a picture. But she heard the camera's click and trod off into the tall grass, moving toward the river to the north. Soon I heard the bell-like alarm call of a sambar she must have surprised. By her radio signal I could tell she kept walking into a patch of gallery forest, then into the tall grass beyond it.

Night settled quickly over the landscape. As I sat in the dark, I reflected on what I had just seen and all that I had learned from tigress 101 in the short month since we attached her radio collar. And I was to learn much more in the months ahead. What we observed of the behavior of tigress 101 in these early days of the Tiger Ecology Project predicted what subsequent research would reveal.

In the first month we followed her, 101 had been using an area of about 6 sq km (2.3 sq miles), expanding later to about 9 sq km (3.5 sq miles) of this thick, rich floodplain habitat. She didn't use every part of that area, but regularly used roads and trails as travel lanes and she used predictable spots to cross streams and roads and to pass between rivers. She did not enter the open agricultural areas that abutted her territory on the east. She had two, 7- or 8-month-old cubs that sometimes followed her on her rounds; other times, she stashed them in thicket hiding places.

By checking on her several times each day, I found that when she made a kill she came back to it for two to three days before moving on. She was making a kill every 5 to 6 days, doing a little better than the average of a kill once every eight days that Melvin Sunquist later found for tigers in Chitwan.

We also determined that tigress 101 had variable periods of activity and movement from one day to the next. Near dusk, she became active and would remain so through most of the night. After sunrise, her activity dropped off. On some days, her transmitter indicated that she did not move about much during the daytime heat, spending her time in a "day bed" in reed thickets, usually close to or even in water. She usually changed day beds from one day to the next, but would return to a particular day bed in later days. During the months I followed her, the distance between her successive day bed sites was from 1 to 2 km (0.6 to 1.2 miles). Occasionally, however, she was up and about during the day. This pattern proved typical of Chitwan tigers. They tend to be most active at night and less active during the mid-day heat, but more active during the cool season than during the hottest time of the year. But this activity pattern is not rigidly fixed. Different prey species tend to vary their activity and movement patterns and tigers respond to them by changing their own activity and movement patterns. Active prey are apparently easier to find and stalk and tigers seem to be able to assess changes in prey activity and respond accordingly.

The pattern I saw in tigress 101 suggested that she matched her activity to seasonal changes in the availability and activity of prey. Each day, just before sunset, when prey were becoming active as the heat of the sun abated, 101 moved from her day bed area to what I called her foraging area, which might be more than 2 km (1.2 miles) away. She covered this distance rapidly and largely directly, using both trails and roads as if they

*The great strength and power of tigers allows them to hunt
and kill animals much larger than themselves. A 250 kg (550 lb) tiger
can take a 1000 kg (2,200 lb) gaur.*

were highways. But while she moved quickly she was also alert to signs of potential prey. Following her tracks in the road dust, I saw she left the road many times and moved into thick roadside cover; at the point where she emerged her tracks were mixed with those of axis deer – ones who'd gotten away!

The relatively short distance a tiger travels from day bed to foraging area is, however, just the beginning of a tiger's nightly forays. George Schaller estimated that a tiger travelled a total of 16 –32 km (10 – 20 miles) during a night of unsuccessful hunting in Kanha National Park in central India, while Sunquist estimated a tiger might travel 10 – 20 km (6 – 12 miles) per night in Chitwan. Again, observations of tigress 101 explain this.

Once tigress 101 arrived in a foraging area, her movement changed from a quick, direct travel mode to a slower, more deliberate hunting mode in which she carefully crossed and criss-crossed the area. When I detected this change in travel mode via radio tracking, I tried to get ahead of her to see her in action. Once, about mid-day, I located her in a patch of tall reeds but when I looked for her in the late afternoon I found her some distance away in a scrub-grass area near the south bank of the Rapti River. From elephant-back I could see a cattle herder slowly moving his cattle north and homeward through the scrub. The cattle were casually feeding on the grass as they headed toward the river bank. At the same time, I could hear a strong signal from 101's transmitter, indicating she was nearby. Suddenly there was a loud burst of activity pulses on the radio, then the death rattle of a throttled bullock. I saw the herder calm his frightened cattle and urge them quickly away. I realised that 101 had timed her movements that day to match the predictable homeward progress of the domestic herd. Later in the season, I found that 101 changed both her activity times and her foraging areas in response to fires that burned throughout the park and reduced much of the tall-grass areas to scattered stalks and ashes. After the fires, sambar confined their activity to the gallery forest on the flood plain, and 101 concentrated on hunting in this "profitable" area. The key to a tigress's success – to live and rear cubs – is to know

Tigers retire to shady day beds during the hottest part of the day, when prey are also resting.

where and when to find food.

The morning after 101 killed the bullock, we rode our elephants to the kill site so we could safely examine the remains. We also wanted to read the sign (tracks and other evidence in the dust and grass) to piece together what had happened overnight. The tigress, and, as we found, her two cubs had moved on to a day bed area by the time we arrived. She had pulled what remained of the bullock into a thick patch of brush. Even so, scavengers had already been busy. Our approach flushed several white-backed vultures from their meal. A group of wild pigs had been feeding at the tiger's kill just before we arrived. From my machan, I had watched wild pigs feed at tiger kills before. The group would come in to feed, apparently sensing that no tiger was present, but they would remain just minutes before moving on. It appeared to me that by remaining in constant motion, the pigs were making it very difficult for a tiger to set and launch an attack on them should it return suddenly to the kill.

While radio-tracking, I had also "watched" tigers return to kills, and it seemed that the tiger would approach a kill site cautiously. I suspected there were two reasons for this. The tiger could potentially surprise and kill a scavenging pig, should one be present. It could also surprise another tiger, which could lead to a deadly fight. Tigers do scavenge the kills of other tigers and other predators when they find them. This trait makes tigers vulnerable to being poisoned by a baited carcass, a method poachers often use to kill them.

The signs showed that 101 had brought her seven-month old cubs to the kill and together they had nearly finished off the bullock, although more usually a tiger might spend two days picking a carcass clean. Tigers usually feed in bouts of an hour or more, then rest, then feed again, on throughout the night. In a night, an adult female might put away nearly 20 kg (44 lb) of meat. Charles McDougal reported that one large male tiger ate 35 kg (77 lb) of meat in a night, but Sunquist found that the average amount of meat eaten by a tiger per night on a kill was between 15 and 18 kg (33 and 40 lb). A tiger typically begins feeding on the hind end of the body and works its way forward. If more than one tiger is feeding on a kill, each starts on a different part of the body.

Tigers rely on the cover of tall grass to stalk unwary prey such as this sambar. Even so, most hunts are unsuccessful.

When they are finished, there is usually nothing left but the skull, a few of the large heavy limb bones, perhaps the spine, a few scraps of hide, and the stomach with its contents intact.

I examined the bullock's neck. The tigress had killed it with a characteristic neck bite. I saw puncture wounds from the tiger's canine teeth on both sides of the bullock's throat, suggesting that the bullock had died of suffocation, but I also noted that its cervical vertebrae (neck bones) were crushed, which is another way a tiger kills its prey.

A typical predatory sequence involves several steps. A tiger: 1. searches for prey; 2. locates prey; 3. approaches to within a distance from which it can launch an attack – the stalk; 4. rushes to the prey; 5. seizes the prey; 6. brings the prey down to the ground; 7. kills the prey with a bite; 8. pulls the prey to a secluded spot; 9. eats it. Seizing, bringing down the prey, and method of killing may vary

When the hunt proves successful, a tiger will feed on prey the size of a sambar for two or three days.

with the size of the prey and the size and experience of the tiger. When a large, experienced tiger kills a smaller prey such as a buffalo calf, the tiger simply grasps the prey by the back of its neck and crushes its neck vertebrae with the canines. Or the tiger may quickly reach under the victim's throat, grab it with the canines and hold on until the prey suffocates. Sometimes the tiger does both.

A larger prey animal requires more skill and effort. The neck of larger prey such as male sambar and gaur (a species of wild cattle in which males may reach 1,000 kg or about 2,200 lb) is much too thick for a tiger's canines to penetrate to the cervical vertebrae, so the tiger must put itself in position to reach the throat to strangle it. For these large prey, the tiger closes quickly, then in rapid-fire sequence, grasps the prey with its sharply clawed forepaws, gets its forequarters onto the prey's back, and reaches down and around to grab the prey's throat in its jaws. The canine teeth puncture each side of the trachea. The tiger then rears back and pulls the prey off its feet, keeping the prey's sharp, flailing hooves pointing away. The tiger maintains its stranglehold for several minutes until the prey ceases to struggle. These are rather complicated movement sequences and there is always the chance that a hoof or horn might connect and render the tiger a crippling blow. Younger tigers practice their prey killing using this complicated sequence on smaller, less dangerous prey.

McDougal and I studied, in detail, the movement sequences tigers use to kill. It was apparent that the tiger, like a martial arts master, uses the prey's own motion to bring it down. The tiger does not leap onto its prey's back, as depicted in so many illustrations, and it does not commit itself to a movement until after the prey does. When the prey makes its move to escape, the tiger rushes in. Tigers keep all four feet on or as close to the ground as long as possible. If it is possible to seize the prey with just jaws and canines, the tiger does so. But if the prey is too large for this approach, the tiger uses the series of movements described above to seize the prey and bring it into position for delivering the killing bite. Speed, strength, retractile claws for gripping and clinging, short, powerful jaws with canine teeth for killing, all put into motion and rendered effective through these behavioral sequences is what being a predatory tiger is all about.

Wherever they live today, tigers are the largest land-living carnivores that depend entirely on a diet of meat (some bears may be larger but their diets are more varied). Tigers specialise in killing large deer, wild cattle, or wild pigs. Wherever tigers occur, so do wild pigs and one or more large deer; through much of their range in south Asia, wild cattle are also important prey. Tigers can kill prey ranging in size from the large males of the wild cattle species, which top the scales at 1,000 kg (about 2,200 lb), to the diminutive muntjacs weighing just 15 kg (33 lb). But several investigators have found that tigers select the largest prey available. The small (and now extinct) Javan tiger – with

A tiger stealthily approaches to within 10 to 20 meters (30 to 60 feet) of prey,
then explodes into a rush. With blinding speed it closes the gap, and with carefully timed
maneuvers delivers a killing neck bite.

males weighing just 100 kg (220 lb) – were reported to regularly prey on bantang (a wild cattle species) and killed bull bantang weighing more than 800 kg (1760 lb)!

In Chitwan, McDougal and I analysed the remains of prey in tiger faeces (called scats) to see if tigers there exhibited such prey selection. We compared how often various prey remains were found in the scats to how "available" each species was to tigers in that habitat. We found that tigers killed wild pigs weighing between 90 and 230 kg (about 200 and 500 lb) and large sambar more often than you would expect based on these species' availability in the park, and killed smaller muntjac and hog deer less often than expected. Axis deer were killed about as often as you would expect. This means that tigers were selecting, perhaps going out of their way to take the larger pigs and sambar, killing axis deer if they ran into them, and sometimes ignoring the smaller hog deer and muntjac. Average prey size for these tigers was about 100 kg (220 lb).

In Nagarahole National Park in south India, Ullas Karanth and Sunquist found that tigers preferred gaur and generally selected prey weighing more than 176 kg (388 lb), with tiger predation biased toward adult male axis deer, sambar, and young gaur.

Just how many prey animals does a tiger kill in a year? While she was accompanied by young cubs, tigress 101 killed about every 5 to 6 days, which would amount to 60 to 70 or so kills a year by a female supporting growing cubs. Later in Chitwan, Sunquist found that, on average, tigers make a kill once every 8 to 8.5 days, or roughly 40 to 50 kills a year. Tigers have to kill more often when their kills are scavenged by villagers, as they are in Chitwan.

Scientists working in a variety of habitats across the tiger's large range have found fairly consistent relationships between the number of tigers and the number of prey animals in a particular area. In habitats where reliable figures are available, such as in Chitwan and Nagarahole each year all of the tigers in that habitat kill from 8 to 10 per cent of the "standing prey biomass," which is jargon for the total weight of the living prey animals in the habitat. To put it very simply, if ten, 100 kg (220 lb) deer (and no other prey species) live in a square kilometer, for a standing prey biomass equal to 1000 kg (2200 lb), one of them (10 per cent of 1000 = one 100 kg/220 lb deer), will be eaten by a tiger. Interestingly, similar 8 to 10 per cent predator-prey ratios have been found in other species and habitats, such as the Serengeti and the South American rainforest. The bottom line is that prey will always vastly outnumber predators.

Not surprisingly, the number of tigers in an area (tiger density) varies directly with the number of prey animals. In the grasslands and forests of Chitwan, prey biomass is about 2500 kg per km (about 14,200 lb per mile), and tiger density is 2.8 to 3.7 per 100 sq km (39 sq miles). In south India's Nagarahole, prey biomass reaches 7700 kg per sq km (about 43,800 lb per sq mile), and correspondingly, tiger density is 11.6 per 100 sq km (39 sq miles). These are very good habitats for prey species and so also for tigers. Prey are far less abundant in the rain forests of Java and the temperate deciduous forests of the Russian Far East. Studies of the Javan tiger in the 1930s found just 500 kg (1100 lbs) of prey per square kilometer of rain forest and 0.75 to 1 tiger per 100 sq km (39 sq miles). In the Russian Far East, there are only 0.2 tigers per 100 sq km (39 sq miles), so while we await the conclusions of studies now underway, we can safely predict that prey numbers are very low indeed. What this variation shows is that there is no simple formula for determining how big an area must be set aside to support a population of tigers. What works in one habitat may not work in another. Such basic information as which prey species live in an area and in what numbers is essential to designing tiger conservation plans that will succeed in saving the tiger.

You will see in the next chapter how, if left alone, the tiger's territorial land-tenure system keeps tiger density in a particular area relatively constant. But density does vary with the quality of the habitat, which depends largely on numbers of prey. As a group, tigers do not overeat their food supply. As individuals, however, they do respond and take advantage of the spots where prey are most abundant, such as the edges of parks where people bring their livestock to graze. Eventually, these edge habitats will degrade under this grazing pressure and the number of wild prey species will diminish. This leads almost inevitably to tigers taking more and more livestock – and villagers demanding that tigers be removed from their midst. This continuing conflict between tigers, the people who live near them, and tiger conservation efforts remains to be resolved.

Family Life

A tiger lives its life in distinct stages. It is born helpless and mobile, utterly dependent on its mother and her milk, a period lasting about two months. Next, the cub begins to mature but remains dependent on its mother as it travels with her, eats at her kills, and plays with the other cubs in the litter. In the next phase, the young tiger is independent of its mother, but stays in her territory as it continues to learn the ropes of being a tiger, exploring the habitat and learning to be a good predator. But then, at about two years of age, it must set off on its own to find a territory for itself. For females, this means an area where she can find enough food to support herself and her future cubs. For males, this area must also include the territories of females whose cubs he hopes to father. This may take a long time. Once on a territory, mating occurs, and a female will enter the cub-rearing phase of her life while a male works to keep other males at bay. Finally, the tiger might spend its last days homeless, having lost its territory and unable to acquire another one. This stage is generally quite short.

At every step of a tiger's way, danger lurks, even for this greatest of cats. Of every 100 tigers born, perhaps 50 do not live to the independent stage. Cubs die in fires set by villagers. They may be eaten by a leopard while their mother is off hunting. They may starve or die of disease. They may even be killed by another tiger.

Of the 50 who do make it to independence, 30 may not survive to establish a territory and begin to produce young. This dispersal stage, as it is called, may the riskiest time of all. At this time, tigers are still honing their hunting skills and are more likely to suffer fatal injuries in a hunting accident than more mature adults. What's more they are travelling and spending time in unfamiliar terrain as they seek a place to settle down. But the best places in a particular area are generally already taken, so these tigers find themselves on the fringes of that area, caught between people living on one side and fiercely territorial tigers on the other. These tigers often take to eating livestock, and risk being killed outright or poisoned by eating a baited carcass. On the other side, challenging a territory holder is also very risky. A fight between animals as well armed as tigers may leave the loser with injuries severe enough to kill it.

Even for the 20 tigers who live to establish a territory, the danger is not past. Hunting accidents remain a possibility. Throughout its life, a tiger may succumb to a disease such as rabies or distemper. Its prey may also succumb to an epidemic disease, perhaps spread from livestock, and the tiger may starve. And there will be constant challenges from other tigers trying to find a territory. Adult males face the greatest risks in this regard because a male fights both for a place to feed and hunt and for mating rights with the females whose territories a male's encompasses. As a result, males apparently do not live as long as females do in the wild. Finally, a tiger lucky enough to live to old age faces starvation as its hunting ability wanes, or death at the hands of other tigers it can no longer defend itself against. On top of all of this "natural" mortality, powerful tigers die at the hands of humans – hunters and poachers as well as villagers trying to protect their own lives and their livestock. This last is "extra" mortality, which the tiger's reproductive rate – how often cubs are produced that survive to produce cubs of their own – fails to keep up with, leading to a decrease in the number of tigers over time.

This, in broad outline, is the life of a tiger. The details of the tiger's social and family life are no less fascinating. In fact, the amassing of a detailed biography of one tigress in Chitwan National Park revealed much of the tiger story.

Charles McDougal began to follow this tigress in 1972 and didn't stop until she died in 1987 at more than 15 years old. Her name was Chuchchi, meaning pointed toes, for the distinctive track she left with a slightly deformed hind foot. I first met this tigress in 1974. She had ended her dispersal phase and was settling into a territory, the boundaries of which she was still working out with a neighboring, older female named 122. Chuchchi lived on this territory, or parts of it, throughout her breeding life. But beginning in 1975 she had many different males in her life. The first male to occupy a territory that overlapped Chuchchi's was 102, who lasted two years. He was replaced by 105, who held the area for three years before SB took over for the next two years. Then there was a period of upheaval. For six months no male entered the vacant territory; then two males – 123 and 127 – arrived almost simultaneously. In the ensuing fight over possession, 123 was killed. Male 127's victory was short lived, however. Just a few months later, male KB ousted 127 and then retained the area for three years until BB, the last of Chuchchi's males, arrived and stayed for the next and last two breeding years of her life.

Chuchchi's first litter of cubs was born in mid-1975, her last in mid-1985. In those ten years, she produced a total of 16 known cubs in five litters. Eleven cubs survived at least until they dispersed at about two years of age, although none of her last litter is believed to have survived. At least three of the various males actually fathered cubs with her; some probably killed the cubs of other males; some undoubtedly did both.

We learned from Chuchchi that adult female tigers often remain near their mothers and some even acquire territories from their mothers. A female from Chuchchi's 1977 litter settled next to her in 1979. About two years later, Chuchchi gave up about half of her territory to a daughter born in 1979. Finally, a daughter born in 1982

Litter-mate tiger cubs enjoy each other's company – playing, resting, even swimming together until beginning an adult tiger's solitary life.

never left. Instead, she drove her mother off in late 1986 just before she produced her own first cubs in early 1987. In the next – and last – few months of her life, Chuchchi took some long, wandering trips to places she was never known to have visited before. But she kept returning "home" until she was finally killed by a young male tiger – the son of her old neighbor, female 122. She was at least 15 and a half years old, her badly worn canines explaining her skeleton-thin condition.

Tigers can give birth at any time of the year, but there is an increase in behaviors related to mating from November to April (the cool season and the early part of the hot season) on the Indian subcontinent. A tigress in estrus (ready to mate) advertises her condition by roaring more at night, and sometimes during the day. She also urine sprays and rubs her body against trees and other objects more often than at other times. Odour chemicals in these sprays and rubs sends a message about her condition to a male who sniffs them. When a male answers her "call" and the two meet, the male displays his larger size but she does not immediately let him too near. The tension is high while the male follows and circles her, slowly closing the distance between them. This male and female are not strangers. Their territories overlap and they regularly communicate through scents and calls. But they seldom meet face to face and only do so warily. Armed with such lethal weapons, a miscue could lead to injury or death.

When the female permits, the pair lick and rub each other. Finally the tigress assumes a special crouching posture called lordosis, signalling her readiness. The male mounts her and pinches the back of her neck in his incisors as they copulate. It is over quickly. She ends it with a yowling call and the male must jump away before the female can bat him with her forepaw. This may be repeated tens, even hundreds of times during the seven or so days she remains in estrus. Many such mating bouts, however, do not result in a viable pregnancy. If one does not, the process will be repeated when the female comes back into estrus in about 40 to 45 days.

Gestation lasts about 102 days. Before giving birth, a tigress selects a secluded birthing site in very thick cover. A Bengal tigress may produce as many as seven cubs in a litter, but most typical is two or three, with an equal number of male and female cubs overall. For the first two months the cubs stay put, unless the female carries them, the scruff of their neck between her teeth, one at a time, to another site. After 11 days or so, their eyes now open, the cubs are capable of crawling away into the thick cover and can even escape a slow-moving grass fire. The tigress comes and goes to hunt, and may be gone for more than 24 hours at a time. The mother first starts taking her cubs to kills or even bringing smaller kills to the cub's vicinity when they are 3 to 4 months old. Soon after, they are regularly at her kills, but the cubs still hide while the tigress is hunting. At this age, cubs play predator, using each other as mock prey during bouts of back straddling, pawing, and biting.

Adult tigers generally come together only to mate.
Even then, male and female treat each other with the utmost caution
in case a wrong move leads to lethal combat.

They also play aggressively, biting, pawing, wrestling, and licking. All of this is good practice for their future.

After one year of age, cubs accompany the tigress nearly full time. The cubs may go out on their own and sometimes attempt to make kills but they remain dependent on their mother. By 18 months or so, when they have their permanent canines, they are moving independently of their mother, though siblings may, but don't always, stay together until they are about two years old. During this period of semi-independence, the tigress may come into estrus again and mate. By 24 months the female may have new cubs and within a month or so her older cubs are truly off on their own.

As noted earlier, newly independent tigers face a tough world. They may move tens of kilometers away from their birth site, through unfamiliar terrain, and encounter some very unfriendly tigers along the way. And in modern landscapes, they may be confined in their movement. David Smith found that tigers will not cross through open agricultural areas, limiting their ability to search for greener pastures beyond. This fact of tiger behavior must be a consideration in the design of reserves for tigers and predicts the problems that will emerge as tiger habitats become islands in a sea of human development.

Smith also found that, from a tiger's point of view, young males spend considerable time in very poor areas . From this tenuous base, the males make repeated forays, looking for a vacant territory or for a territory with females and food that is possessed by a male which the younger one might successfully challenge. In contrast, females focus their search in areas of prime habitat, with the survivors often settling near or taking over part of their mother's territory.

The way adult tigers space themselves out, the size of the territories they secure for themselves, and how strongly they defend those territories did not arise by chance. The essential resource that a territory provides is food. But not only must prey be present, and present in sufficient numbers, it must also be catchable. That means that there must be enough cover for the tiger to hunt from: an open prairie covered with buffalo is an empty wasteland to a tiger that depends on stealth to stalk its prey.

For female tigers, food, enough for herself and her cubs, is the only consideration.

Once established on a territory where she can find and catch enough prey in a timely fashion to support herself and her cubs, she jealously keeps all other adult females out. Male tigers, in addition to food, must focus on the availability of females to mate with. A male's territory usually overlaps that of one to seven females, and he must defend this large area from all other adult males or be replaced as the breeding male. For males, the rule of "the more females the better" is true only up to a point. The male must use and actively patrol all parts of his territory on a regular basis, or the unused parts may be taken over by a new male or annexed into the territory of a neighboring male.

What's more, the male must also keep other male tigers away from the cubs he has fathered – his only role in raising them. Adult male tigers are a real danger to cubs not their own – they kill them. A tigress completely avoids all males while she is rearing cubs and may even abandon a kill to a male rather than expose her cubs to his threatening presence. (Observations of known tigers in central India show that sometimes a female and her cubs will share a kill or a favorite water hole with an adult male. In these cases, the cubs are likely his, and the female knows the male well enough to "handle" him.) For a male to succeed at all in leaving surviving young, he, too, must keep other males away. This limits a male's territory to a defensible size. Still, as the males in Chuchchi's life demonstrated, the tenure of a territorial male is relatively brief – two to three years – compared to that of females.

Obviously, male territories will always be bigger than those of females. But the absolute size of tiger territories varies immensely within habitats and over the tiger's range, depending on, once again, the availability of prey. In prey-rich Chitwan, female territories range in size from 10 to 51 sq km (about 4 to 20 sq miles), male from 19 to 151. In the Sumatran rain forest, with less abundant prey, females defend between 90 and 190 sq km, males between 180 and 380. And in the prey-poor Soviet Far East, these numbers are 100 to 400 sq km (39 to 156 sq miles) for females and 800 to 1000 sq km (312 to 390 sq miles) for males.

The final fight between two adult males vying for a territory can be brutally violent; the loser may die from its wounds. But any encounter between two tigers is fraught with

Cubs hidden in a cave guarded by their mother
find refuge from such potential predators as leopards and people.
About half of tiger cubs do not survive to independence.

*Sniffing a scent mark left by another tiger, this female may
learn about that tiger's sex and perhaps its identity. Communicating remotely
allows tigers to avoid dangerous face-to-face encounters.*

danger, so both males and females spend a lot of time avoiding each other. Roaring is one means of avoidance. To hear a tiger roaring, the deep call echoing through the night, is an awesome, thrilling experience. To other tigers, it says, Here I am, Here I am, Here I am, warning them to stay away. This long-distance call is made by all of the *Panthera* cats. Tigers roar while moving about on their daily rounds. After making a kill, a tiger might make a short inspection of the vicinity and roar. Movies to the contrary, tigers do not roar before launching and during an attack on prey.

Apart from roaring, most of a tiger's territorial defense behaviors are covert. Tigers place olfactory, or scent, clues, often combined with visual signals, to send a message to other tigers. This is called marking. Olfactory clues are found in urine and faeces, and are produced in the secretions of various glands on the tiger's body. These marks may convey several messages: I've been here and how long ago; I am male or female; I am coming into estrus or not; I am a stranger or a neighbor; even, perhaps, I am a particular tiger.

Smith, McDougal, and Dale Miquelle studied tiger marking using Chuchchi's territory as a focal area. Tigers spray urine, much like house cats do. Both males and females squirt urine on trees and other objects and they tend to concentrate these marks along their territorial boundaries. Generally, males urinate higher on objects (up to 140 cm/55 ins above the ground) and do so more often (2.4 times per km/3.8 times per mile) than females do, but there is overlap. Tigers use their hind feet to scrape shallow depressions in the soil, where they also sometimes urinate and defecate and probably deposit secretions from their anal glands. Tigers rub their cheeks, another site of glands, on objects, frequently on trees they have previously sprayed with urine. Tigers sometimes stand on their hind legs and scrape gouges into trees with their forepaws, and males sometimes flatten vegetation, presumably to call attention to a particular spot.

Tigers mark most frequently when they are first establishing territories and they do so most intensively near territorial boundaries and near frequently used contact points such as crossings. A female marks most frequently just before estrus and her territorial male marks most frequently while she is in estrus. Except for the female's estrus marking, the point of all this marking is the same. Like roaring, it says, I am here, stay away. A tiger cannot be everywhere in its territory at once, so a territory cannot be defended by its physical presence alone. Moreover, it is generally in the interest of other tigers not to wander into another tiger's territory by mistake. Scent marking solves this logistical problem for tigers, as its does for many other mammals.

Most wild cats exhibit a solitary, territorial life style similar to that of tigers. Lions, which live in large social groups, are a significant exception. Several related lionesses – sister, aunts, grandmothers, and daughters – form the core of a lion group. The females, called a pride, defend a group territory against other females and co-operatively raise their cubs. Smaller groups of male lions, called coalitions, come and go in the lives of the pride, much like male tigers come and go in the lives of territorial females. Male coalitions, usually composed of brothers, half-brothers, and cousins, fight other male coalitions for access to female prides. Both male and female lions can and do kill prey on their own, but lion groups, especially female ones, also co-operate in hunting large prey.

Why the social life of lions and tigers, so similar under their coats, is so different has been the subject of considerable discussion and scientific research. For a long time, it was believed that group hunting allowed lions to take more or larger prey so that each lion got more food than if it had hunted alone. But Craig Packer and his associates studying lions in the Serengeti plains of East Africa found this not to be generally true. Instead, they believe that the key to group living in lions is the need to defend large kills from others. In the open habitats – plains and savannas – that lions live in, a single lion on a large kill will quickly attract the attention of other lions as well as other predators and a single lioness will not usually be able to defend her kill. Under these conditions, a lioness' best bet is to share her kill with close relatives, rather than lose it to strangers. The lions group-living social system is based on this advantage.

In contrast, tigers, and most other cats, live in closed habitats: forests, scrub, mangroves, and riverine, tall grasslands, where they hunt and kill with stealth and in secrecy. But still the fabric of their social lives is complex. A solitary tiger, passing along the edge of a jungle clearing or padding down a dusty forest road, is in nearly constant, albeit remote, contact with other tigers in the area. Far from being alone, that tiger lives within a demanding social order and is part of a wider, closely linked community.

Saving the Tiger

I am deeply concerned by the great trouble in tiger-land. We are at a decisive moment in the life of this splendid predator. The tiger, a most cherished symbol of power and grace, has been pushed to the edge of its existence in the wild. Bearing witness to the passing, to the death of tigers in wild Asia, is a horrible experience. I know this experience first hand. I was there at the passing of the Javan tiger.

This is our last chance to save the wild tigers. While the tiger's unbroken range once spanned south and southeast Asia and into the Russian Far East, there has been a virtual collapse in the tiger's geographic range and in tiger numbers in the 50 years since the Second World War. Today, there remain only a few small tracts where we can hope to maintain the vestige of an Asian wildlife heritage, where the tiger can remain part of wild Asia in the face of ever more people and their need for land.

Consider this: Of the eight subspecies, only five remain. The tiger subspecies that once lived in the vicinity of the Caspian Sea is gone; extinct. The Bali Tiger; extinct. The Javan tiger; extinct. The central Chinese tiger has been reduced to just tens of individuals in the wild. The Siberian tiger is reduced to a few hundred individuals. Only 500 or so Sumatran tigers, the last of the island tigers, remain. These last three tiger subspecies are critically endangered. All could blink out and be lost forever in less than a decade, without our immediate and full attention and intensive conservation action. And what of the other two tiger subspecies? The Indo-Chinese tiger, the tiger of Thailand, Cambodia, Malaysia, Vietnam, Laos and Myanmar, has been reduced to 1500 or even fewer. Fewer than 4000 or so Bengal tigers remain in small remnant populations, scattered through the Indian subcontinent. We will lose these wondrous animals in the next decade or two if we do not take up the challenge of saving the tiger with a new and powerful urgency.

The challenge of saving the tiger is at the heart of conservation. The tiger is in trouble. People are responsible for the tiger's plight and only people can ensure the tiger's survival needs are met in the wild so it can survive. Saving the tiger depends on co-ordinated and thoughtful support from all people throughout the world.

Saving the tiger rests on a sophisticated scientific knowledge about the tiger's needs for quality space and adequate prey.

Saving the tiger rests on the well-being of its prey and the forests where they still live, its critical habitat, in blocks large enough to support viable tiger populations.

Saving the tiger rests on the stewardship, the skill, and the dedication of the professionals entrusted with seeking the ways and means for the tiger's survival.

These tiger skins were confiscated in Calcutta, India. Rampant poaching of tigers for their skins, bones, and other parts may be the greatest current threat to this magnificent predator's survival.

Saving the tiger is stopping the killing — the massive haemorrhage in tiger numbers — from human-induced mortality to tiger populations.

Saving the tiger is breaking the economic demand for tiger parts and products that leads people to kill tigers.

Saving the tiger is making tigers and critical tiger habitats positive features in regional land-use and economic advancement programs so that the people that live in tiger lands benefit from the tigers living there.

Saving the tiger depends upon the support of the citizens of the countries where wild tigers still live. Saving the tiger depends upon the support of people everywhere.

Tiger Facts

Common names:

	English:	Tiger
	Hindi:	Bagh, Sher
	Nepali:	Bagh
	Indonesian:	Harimau, Macan
	Malay:	Harimu
	Chinese:	Wu, Lao Hu
	Lao:	Seua
	Vietnamese:	Cop
	Thai:	Seua
	Korean:	Ho Lang-ee

Scientific name:	*Panthera tigris*
Gestation (days):	100-106
Age at maturity (months):	20-24
Longevity (years):	15+ in wild / 20 in zoological parks

Characteristics of the larger mainland tigers, represented by the Bengal tiger, and the smaller island tiger from Sumatra:

		Panthera t. sumatrae Sumatran tiger	*Panthera t. tigris* Bengal tiger
Adult weight (kg / lb):	Male:	100-140 / 220-309	180-258 / 396-569
	Female:	75-110 / 165-242	100-160 / 220-352
Total length (cm / ins):	Male:	220-255 / 86-101	270-310 / 107-122
	Female:	215-230 / 84-90	240-265 / 94-105
Ground coat color:		notably darker	lighter
Color of undersides:		dirty white	clean white
Color of forelegs and throat:		unclearly defined	sharply defined
Stripes:		numerous, closely spaced, may have spots at ends	fewer, widely spaced

Distribution and present numbers

In historical times, the tiger was distributed across most of Asia, but present distribution is very restricted and fragmented. Three of the eight subspecies – Bali tiger, Javan tiger and Caspian tiger – are extinct. The 500 or so remaining Sumatran tigers are restricted to some forest areas on Sumatra. The 3,000-5,300 remaining Bengal tigers are found in some fragmented forests tracts in India, Nepal, Bhutan, Bangladesh, Myanmar, and China. The 900-1,500 Indo-Chinese tigers live in scattered forest tracts in Myanmar, Thailand, Laos, Cambodia, Vietnam, China, and Malaysia. Fewer than 20 Chinese tigers live in southeastern China. The 250-400 Amur or Siberian tigers live in the Russian Far East, with perhaps a few remaining in northeastern China.

Biographical Note

John Seidensticker was raised on a cattle ranch in Montana, U.S.A. and received his B.A. and M.S. degrees from the University of Montana. He pioneered the use of radio-telemetry in the study of large, solitary-living cats and wrote his Ph.D. dissertation on Mountain Lion Social Organization in the Idaho Primitive Area at the University of Idaho. He served as founding principal investigator for the Nepal-Smithsonian Tiger Ecology Project and as an ecologist and park planner for the WWF-Indonesia Programme. Dr. Seidensticker is author or editor of more than 100 papers, articles, and books, and is Curator of Mammals, Smithsonian National Zoological Park, and Chairman of the Save The Tiger Fund Council.

Recommended Reading

Jim Corbett's *Man Eaters of Kumaon*, Oxford University Press, 1944, is an adventure story and sympathetic account of people living in tiger country early last century. Today, tigers have all but disappeared from these hills. George B. Schaller's *The Deer and the Tiger*, University of Chicago Press, 1967, and Charles McDougal's *Face of the Tiger*, Rivington Books and Andre Deutsch, London, 1977, remain essential tiger background reading. Melvin E. Sunquist's *The Social Organization of Tigers in Royal Chitawan National Park*, Smithsonian Contributions to Zoology No. 336, 1981, is a classic monograph based on radio tracking. His work is summarized in F. and M. Sunquist's *Tiger Moon*, University of Chicago Press, 1988. Valmik Thapar's *Tigers, The Secret Life*, Rodale Press, Emmaus PA, 1989, (with photographs by Fateh Singh Rathore) is an account of the problems conservationists encounter in central India. R. Tilson and U.S. Seal, eds. *Tigers of the World: The Biology, Biopolitics, Management, and Conservation of an Endangered Species*, Noyes Press, Park Ridge NJ, 1987, contains technical reports on many aspects of tiger biology and accounts from most areas of the tigers' geographical range. *Great Cats*, John Seidensticker and Susan Lumpkin, eds., Rodale Press, Emmaus PA, 1991, is a comprehensive introduction to all the cats and includes sections on tigers. J.Seidensticker, S.Christie, P. Jackson, eds. *Riding the Tiger: Tiger Conservation in Human-dominated Landscapes*, Cambridge University Press, 1999, brings together the recent thinking and research of 79 tiger conservationists.